CARLOS DELGADO

PAT HENTGEN

JOHN OLERUD

TONY FERNANDEZ

DAVID WELLS

JOE CARTER

GEORGE BELL

TONY BATISTA

ROBERTO ALOMAR

DAVE STIEB

TOM HENKE

ALFREDO GRIFFIN

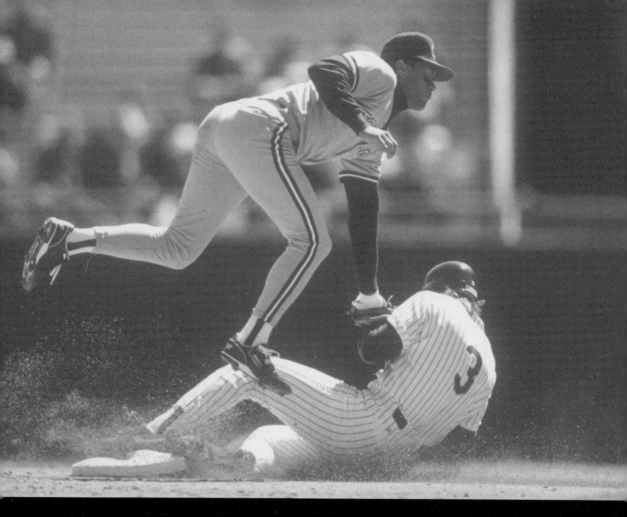

THE HISTORY OF THE
TORONTO
BLUE JAYS

MICHAEL E. GOODMAN

CREATIVE ⬤ EDUCATION

Published by Creative Education, 123 South Broad Street, Mankato, MN 56001

Creative Education is an imprint of The Creative Company.

Designed by Rita Marshall.

Photographs by AllSport (Jim Commentucci, Greg Fiume, Andy Lyons, Rick Stewart), Associated Press/

Wide World Photos, Icon Sports Media (Chuck Solomon), Anthony Neste, SportsChrome

(Jeff Carlick, Rob Tringali Jr., Michael Zito)

Library of Congress Cataloging-in-Publication Data

Goodman, Michael E. The history of the Toronto Blue Jays / by Michael Goodman.

p. cm. — (Baseball)   ISBN 1-58341-227-1

Summary: Highlights the key personalities in the team history of the Toronto Blue Jays,

formed when the American League expanded in 1977.

1. Toronto Blue Jays (Baseball team)—History—

Juvenile literature. [1. Toronto Blue Jays (Baseball team)—History.]

I. Title. II. Baseball (Mankato, Minn.).

GV875.T67 G66 2002   796.357'64'09713541—dc21   2001047877

First Edition 9 8 7 6 5 4 3 2 1

LONG BEFORE

EUROPEANS ARRIVED IN NORTH AMERICA, THE HURON

Indians had a favorite spot for tribal meetings along the shores of what is now Lake Ontario. They called the place To'ron'to, which meant "place of meeting" in their language. In the 1600s, French settlers established a mission and fur-trading post on the site and eventually built a fort there. Toronto passed into British hands following the French and Indian War and became the capital of the province of Upper Canada (now Ontario).

Twice during the War of 1812, armies from the United States invaded Toronto. More than 160 years later, in 1977, another type of invasion occurred when teams from the American League (AL) began arriving in Toronto to battle baseball's newest expansion

DOUG AULT

team—the Toronto Blue Jays. The Blue Jays quickly established a loyal fan base and a winning legacy in the North.

In **1977**, third baseman Roy Howell set a team record by driving in nine runs in one game.

{STARTING OUT SLOWLY} The Toronto Blue Jays joined the American League in 1977 along with the Seattle Mariners. From the beginning, the Blue Jays decided to stress youth and to focus on building a strong minor-league system. Toronto management asked fans to be patient, promising that although it might take a while to create a winner, it would be worth the wait. The club did indeed suffer growing pains, finishing last in the AL Eastern Division in its first five seasons.

Despite the losses, there was still plenty of excitement in Exhibition Stadium, the Blue Jays' first home. The excitement actually began on opening day—April 7, 1977—when rookie first baseman Doug Ault slammed two home runs to lead the Jays to a

ALEX GONZALEZ

Swift short-stop Alfredo Griffin starred as Toronto's leadoff hitter from **1979** to **1982**.

ALFREDO GRIFFIN

9–5 win over the Chicago White Sox. Another highlight was a late-season 19–3 slaughter of the New York Yankees, as the Blue Jays scored more runs than any other opposing team in Yankee Stadium in 50 years.

Standouts on the first Toronto squad included Ault, shortstop Bob Bailor, third baseman Roy Howell, and pitchers Dave Lemanczyk and Jerry Garvin. The club ended its first season with a league-worst 54–107 record, but more than 1.7 million people attended Blue Jays home games—a sign that Toronto fans were both enthusiastic and patient.

That patience was rewarded in 1979 with the arrival of two outstanding young athletes: hard-hitting shortstop Alfredo Griffin and power pitcher Dave Stieb. Griffin was voted the AL co-Rookie of the Year in 1979 when he set club records for hits (179), runs scored (81), triples (10), and stolen bases (21). In addition, his .279

Brawny first baseman John Mayberry led the offense with 30 homers and 82 RBI in **1980**.

9

JOHN MAYBERRY

Like Alfredo Griffin, Jays up-and-comer Felipe Lopez was a standout at shortstop.

FELIPE LOPEZ

batting average was the best among all AL shortstops.

Stieb, meanwhile, provided his own fireworks on the mound.

Second base-
man Damaso
Garcia led
the team
in batting
average in
both **1980**
and **1982**.
In 1977, Stieb had been an outfielder at Southern Illinois University. Toronto scouts had gone to see him hit and were not very impressed. Then, by chance, Stieb's coach had called on him to pitch a few innings in relief that afternoon. When the scouts saw

the young man's sizzling fastball, they were amazed. "He was absolutely overpowering," said Bobby Mattick, one of the scouts. "We hadn't liked him as a hitter, but he sure opened our eyes when he started pitching."

The Blue Jays chose Stieb in the amateur draft following the 1978 season. He stayed in the minors for only half a season and was promoted to Toronto by July 1979. Between 1979 and 1992, Stieb set most of the Blue Jays' pitching records, winning 174 games,

DAVE STIEB

hurling 30 shutouts, striking out more than 1,600 batters, and main-

taining a 3.42 ERA. He was elected to the AL All-Star team seven

times, pitched the only no-hitter in Blue Jays history in 1990, and

had three other potential no-hitters broken up in the ninth inning.

Despite the efforts of Griffin, Stieb, and other young stars such

as second baseman Damaso Garcia, first baseman Willie Upshaw, and pitcher Jim Clancy, the Blue Jays could not escape the AL East cellar. Still, the club began edging closer and closer to the .500 level,

and Toronto fans believed that the Blue Jays would be a winner very soon.

{THE WINNING STREAK BEGINS} In 1982, two major changes occurred in Toronto. First, veteran manager Bobby Cox took over as the team's field general, bringing with him a new winning attitude. Next, center fielder Lloyd Moseby and right fielder Jesse Barfield began to emerge as potential stars. The next year, George Bell arrived in Toronto to fill the third outfield spot, and one of the top outfield combinations in recent baseball history was in place—and ready to post some winning numbers.

The three stars were closely matched. In fact, they were all born within 15 days of each other in 1959 and had come up

LLOYD MOSEBY

together through the Blue Jays' minor-league system. Moseby was the first to show his star power in the big leagues. In 1983, he batted .315, had 81 RBI, and stole 27 bases. And his defense may

have been even better than his offense. "With that guy in center field," said Cleveland Indians manager Pat Corrales, "anything in the outfield can be caught."

Barfield also began to shine in 1983, pounding a team-high

27 home runs and patrolling right field with speed and a great arm.

Bell took a little longer to develop but soon became

the best of the three. In 1983, the young stars led the

Blue Jays to an 89–73 record, their first winning

campaign. Cox was proud of his players and

promised fans a division title soon.

One of baseball's best defensive outfielders, Jesse Barfield spent nine seasons in Toronto.

Toronto fans had a short wait. By 1985, it was obvious that

the Blue Jays were the top team in the AL East. In addition to

Stieb and their fabulous outfield, the Jays featured shortstop

Tony Fernandez, a speedy switch-hitter with great range in the field,

and top relievers Tom Henke and Dennis Lamp. Toronto assumed

possession of first place in the division early in the season and never

gave it up. By season's end, the Blue Jays' record stood at 99–62,

the best mark in club history.

JESSE BARFIELD

With 203 career round-trippers, outfielder Joe Carter became Toronto's home run king.

The Blue Jays, who had gone from worst to first in the AL East

in just three seasons, were favored to beat the Kansas City Royals in

the AL Championship Series (ALCS) and in fact won

three of the first four games. Then the Royals

destroyed the Jays' hopes by winning three straight

games to claim the AL pennant.

{BELL RINGS IN MVP NUMBERS} Following the

20 successful 1985 season, Cox stepped down as Toronto's manager

and was replaced by third-base coach Jimy Williams. The team was

slow to respond to Williams and wound up in fourth place with an

86–76 record. The biggest problem in 1986 was pitching. Stieb lost

his first six games and finished 7–12, and only lefty Jimmy Key was

a consistent winner.

But while the pitching was substandard, the hitting was

tremendous. Barfield led the AL in home runs with 40, and Bell

GEORGE BELL

cracked 31 more. Fernandez also set a team record with 213 hits. All

three Toronto standouts were named to the AL All-Star team.

Bell truly came into his own in 1987 and almost carried the

Blue Jays to another division title. The slugger from the Dominican

Republic set club records with 47 homers and 134 RBI while

batting .308 and scoring 111 runs. For his sensational performance,

Bell was voted the AL Most Valuable Player (MVP).

The Jays topped the AL East again in 1989. Playing in their

In a **1989** game, infielder Kelly Gruber hit for the cycle (a single, double, triple, and home run).

fabulous new home, the Skydome, the Jays opened the year 12–24—a terrible start that led the club to bring in Cito Gaston as its new manager—but bounced back to finish the year 89–73. Bell, Barfield, and first baseman Fred McGriff provided the power, while

Stieb, Key, and newcomers David Wells and Todd Stottlemyre formed a tough pitching rotation.

In the ALCS, the Jays fell to the powerhouse Oakland Athletics, the eventual World Series champs, four games to one. Jays fans were disappointed but certain that their club would finally reach the top in the 1990s.

{FLYING HIGH IN THE '90S} The club won another division title in 1991 and lost another ALCS. Still, fans poured into

KELLY GRUBER

Big pitcher David Wells was a late-**1980s** standout who returned in the late '**90s**.

DAVID WELLS

the Skydome all season to see the high-flying Jays, and Toronto became the first major-league team ever to attract more than 4 million fans to its home games in one season.

The club made a three-part promise to its fans the next year: "We Can" (defend our division title); "We Are" (going to capture our first AL pennant); "We Will" (win our first World Series). In the end, the Blue Jays did all three. Thanks to the strong pitching of Jack Morris and Juan Guzman and the timely hitting of second baseman Roberto Alomar, first baseman John Olerud, and outfielder Joe Carter, the Jays won the AL East again, defeated the A's 4–2 in the ALCS, and earned Canada's first appearance in the World Series, facing off against the Atlanta Braves.

The series was a nail-biter. The Jays went up three games to two with a chance to close out the Braves in game six. That contest

First baseman John Olerud batted .308 in the **1992** World Series to help Toronto win the title.

JOHN OLERUD

went into extra innings, when outfielder Dave Winfield drove in

two runs to put Toronto ahead. Atlanta rallied but fell just short,

4–3, and the Blue Jays were world champions at last. "What an

honor it is to be part of this team," said Winfield. "This means an

awful lot to the people of Canada. I'm just so happy we could make

it happen for them."

The Blue Jays' momentum carried over into the 1993 season. Several former stars were gone, including Stieb, but Olerud, designated hitter Paul Molitor, and Alomar finished the season 1-2-3 in batting in the AL to propel the Jays to a second straight AL pennant.

In another exciting World Series, the Jays topped the Philadelphia Phillies, four games to two, to win a second consecutive championship. In game six, the Blue Jays came from behind in one of the most dramatic finishes in World Series history, winning 8–6 when Carter slammed a "walk off" homer in the bottom of the ninth inning.

{DELGADO POURS ON THE POWER} After their back-to-back championships, the Blue Jays slipped in the AL East standings. The club's 11-year winning streak came to an end in 1994. Then, starting in 1995, the Jays began a serious rebuilding campaign. Over

In his one and only season in a Blue Jays uniform (**1992**), Dave Winfield knocked in 91 runs.

DAVE WINFIELD

the next few years, fan favorites such as Carter, Alomar, and

Olerud left town and were replaced by new stars such as pitcher

In a **1998** game against Kansas City, ace Roger Clemens fanned a franchise-record 18 batters.

Pat Hentgen, who won the 1996 AL Cy Young Award;

outfielders Shawn Green and Shannon Stewart;

shortstop Alex Gonzalez; and first baseman

Carlos Delgado. These new players helped put the

Jays back on the winning track.

28

Several veterans also made brief but memorable stays in

Toronto in the late 1990s, such as slugging outfielder Jose Canseco

and fireballing pitcher Roger Clemens. Canseco crushed 46 home

runs in his only season in Toronto (1998), and Clemens followed up

Hentgen's Cy Young season with two of his own in 1997 and 1998,

going 41–13 over those two years. Clemens was then traded to the

Yankees before the 1999 season for lefty David Wells, a former

Toronto pitcher who became the new ace of the squad.

ROGER CLEMENS

Jays teams in the late '90s featured more than just strong pitching, however. Green, shortstop Tony Batista, and catcher Darrin Fletcher provided a serious power surge at the Skydome. Yet none of them could match the numbers put up by Delgado. Between 1997 and 2001, the Puerto Rican strongman swatted 30 or more home runs each year. In 1998, he also became the first player ever to homer into the fifth deck of right field at the Skydome. The incredible shot traveled nearly 500 feet. But then again, as Blue Jays outfielder Dave Martinez said, "Carlos has never hit a ball soft."

Outfielder Shawn Green put together a 28-game hitting streak in **1999**, the AL's longest.

Delgado was chosen to play in the All-Star Game in both 2000 and 2001, won the Silver Slugger award as the AL's best hitting first baseman in both 1999 and 2000, and placed high in the voting for league MVP in 2000. He also quickly became a legend on both sides of the border and the dread of pitchers throughout the AL.

SHAWN GREEN

Power hitter Carlos Delgado drove in 100-plus runs every year from **1998** to **2001**.

CARLOS DELGADO

A great fastball hitter, right fielder Raul Mondesi was also known for his rifle arm.

RAUL MONDESI

In little more than 25 years of existence, the Toronto Blue Jays

have brought two world championships north of the U.S. border

Toronto was counting on the pitching contributions of Roy Halladay in **2003** and beyond. and featured some of the game's top players. Since

rising from the bottom of the AL, they have become

one of the league's most consistent winners and made

Toronto's Skydome one of the best "places of meeting"

in all of baseball.

ROY HALLADAY